# THE SINK

## Radical Transformation With One Small Change

D0523096

BY **WALTER NUSBAUM**
AND **DAREN MARTIN**, PHD

The SINK: Radical Transformation with One Small Change

©2016 by Walter Nusbaum and Daren Martin

Published by Clovercroft Publishing, Franklin, Tennessee

Cover and Interior Design by Tamyra McCartney-Burleson

Illustrations by John Pechachek

Conceptual Edits by Tammy Kling

Copy Edit by Lapiz Digital Services and Valerie Johnson

Printed in the United States of America

978-1-942557-88-3

# HOW TO IMPLEMENT
## ONE SIMPLE TECHNIQUE
### THAT WILL BE
# A GAME
# CHANGER
### FOR YOUR PEOPLE
### AND
### PROFITS.

R

# A GIFT
# FROM
# US—

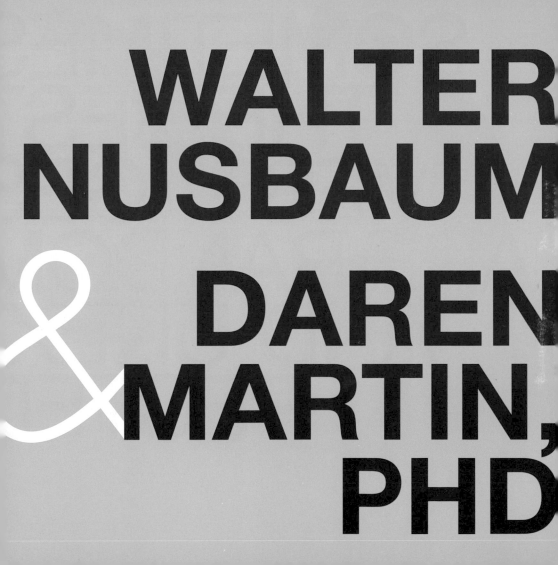

WALTER
NUSBAUM

&DAREN
MARTIN,
PHD

SOMETIMES
THE BEST
MESSAGES
ARE RANDOM
AND UNEX
PECTED

—FROM A
STRANGER

Let everyone sweep in front of his own door, and the whole world will be clean.

— JOHANN WOLFGANG VON GOETHE

When you make the
world a little better,
you advance us all.

– DAREN MARTIN

Never forget that you are one of a kind.
Never forget that if there weren't any need
for you in all your uniqueness on this earth,
you wouldn't be here in the first place.

And never forget, no matter how
overwhelming life's challenges and
problems seem to be, one person
can make a difference in the world.

In fact, it is always because of one
person that all the changes that
matter in the world came about.
So be that one person.

—R. BUCKMINSTER
FULLER

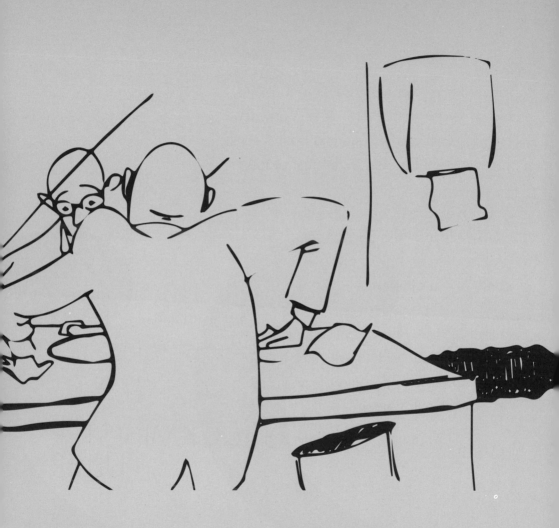

Walking to the sink in an airport restroom, I was
surprised and amused by the scene in front of me.

A polished looking man in a sharp suit was
wiping down the sink with paper towels.

Introducing a little humor, I asked,
"Have you been working here long?"

Returning my smile as he turned to go, the man
said something that changed me forever...

YOU KNOW,
IT'S NOT A BAD IDEA
TO LEAVE THINGS A
**LITTLE BETTER**
THAN HOW YOU
FOUND THEM.

# I WAS STUNNED.

I thought,

# "He's so right!"

As I finished drying my hands, I couldn't help but begin to wipe down my sink.

When I boarded my plane, I settled into my seat and prepared for takeoff. Once we were airborne, the flight attendant moved about the cabin offering drinks and peanuts.

As I stared out the window, the stranger's words at the sink stayed with me....

IT'S NOT A BAD IDEA TO LEAVE THINGS A **LITTLE BETTER** THAN HOW YOU FOUND THEM.

When we landed, I headed for the bathroom
on the way to baggage claim.

STANDING ALONE,
**I FOUND MYSELF DOING
THE SAME THING,**
WIPING DOWN THE SINK WITH
MY FRESHLY USED PAPER
TOWELS...

Once again, the man's words resonated in my head.

27

I began to apply this simple principle to my life when I used public restrooms.

Not just once…

# BUT
# EVERY
# TIME.

# LEAVE THINGS
# **BETTER**
# THAN YOU
# FOUND THEM

THIS simple truth is transformational.

**SMALL IDEAS** that are shared can produce **SIGNIFICANT OUTCOMES.**

**LITTLE ACTIONS** can achieve **BIG RESULTS.**

**AFTER OBSERVING** one lived-out idea, **A NEW HABIT WAS BORN.**

What if I adopted this philosophy of life in everything I do?

What would it look like if everyone left things better than they found them as a way of life?

Our relationships would be…

# STRONGER

# RICHER

# BETTER...

Our work would be…

# MORE FULFILLING

# ENERGIZING

# PROFITABLE...

Our world would be…

On a simple level, leaving things better than you found them may look like...

- Telling someone what you admire about them

- Teaching someone a skill you have

- Passing on a great book

- Refilling the copy paper before it is out

- Sharing a time-saving tip you discovered

- Thoroughly proofing documents

- Picking up trash in front of you

- Planting more flowers in your yard

- Mentoring a child who has no mentors

On a bigger level, leaving things better than you found them may look like…

- Organizing a neighborhood clean-up day

- Financing the education of a student in need

- Writing a book to inspire people

- Improving a time-consuming process

- Coming up with solutions not just fixes

- Coaching a new coworker

- Starting a recycling program at your company

- Taking a trip with a relief organization

- Making your company better

A few years ago, I (Daren) adopted this
as my personal mantra...

amplify
inheren
greatness

# I AMPLIFY THE INHERENT GREATNESS IN EVERYONE I MEET.

That commitment to leaving everyone I encountered better than I found them prompted the following interchange.

I have a large oil and gas client in Wyoming. When I visit Cheyenne, I frequently stop at the same gas station…

This was the conversation one morning

**Me:** "Good morning!!!"

**Two Clerks:** "Good morning!"

**Me:** "By the way, do you know
how important your job is?"

**Two Clerks:** "What are you talking about, dude?
We work at a gas station!"

**Me:** "No seriously! For many people you are the first
human contact they have had all day! The
way you interact with them influences their
thinking throughout their day. You two are
in a very impactful position!"

*The big smile on their faces as I left indicated
they saw their role in a whole new light.*

# THINK ABOUT IT.

What would the world look like if we all left things better than we found them?

Here is a roadmap to make the SINK actionable.

SENSE the need

I NVEST yourself

NULLIFY the need

KEEP it going

# STOP RIGHT NOW

and look around you.

Listen to the sounds around you.

**What are some immediate opportunities to leave things better than you found them?**

SENSE
THE
NEED

Look around you. There are opportunities for improvement, advancement, and cleanup everywhere. Open your senses to what is going on around you and look for where you can make things better.

What can you do to make the world you interact with everyday a more beautiful, functional, comfortable, dynamic, and more engaging place? What opportunities do you have at your workplace to make things better for everyone?

INVEST YOUR-
SELF

Many people sit on the sideline waiting for someone else to take care of things.

## IT'S EASY TO HAVE THE ATTITUDE...

- It's not my job
- I'll get to it later
- I would help but…
- Someone else will take care of it
- Someone else will clean it up
- I did my part, that should be enough

These attitudes don't lead to greatness. The greatest people give their time and talent away to make things better. They invest themselves, their resources, and their energy to make their workplace and world a better place.

Once you set a change in motion, take full responsibility to see it come to fruition.

Like the captain of a ship, navigate through the choppy waters of resistance and inertia. Use the resources around you and inspire the people around you to make things better. You may not do all the work. In fact, it is better if you don't.

## YOUR ROLE IS TO NAVIGATE TO A SUCCESSFUL OUTCOME.

Remember that the needs that seem small to you may be very significant to another person. Don't underestimate the power of a small improvement. Don't stop until you have nullified the need.

# PEOPLE ARE TIRED OF TALK.

# KEEP IT GOING

The SINK principle is a way of life to be shared. You don't just teach it to others; you demonstrate it in ways that make them want to adopt it as a life philosophy.

If the man in the airport had simply droned on about the importance of leaving things better than you found them without demonstrating it by wiping the sink, it would have been just more talk.

Inspire, train, and encourage others to leave things better than they found them by doing it yourself. PAY IT FORWARD.

REME

THE SINK PRINCIPLE MEANS
THERE WILL BE TIMES YOU
WILL NEED TO DO
HARD THINGS.

When we go into organizations to teach this remarkably simple principle, we oftentimes see a culture of entitlement or a "me first" attitude among employees.

After we deliver The SINK One-Day Workshop, we are able to show authentic and tangible examples of excellence and accountability.

In effect,
## CULTURES ARE CHANGED.

What's your personal action plan to leave things better than you found them?

# BE PRO- ACTIVE.

MAKE THE COMMITMENT TODAY.

Gold  Platinum  Silver

# SINK OLYMPICS

**SILVER MEDAL:**
Clean up your own messes

**GOLD MEDAL:**
Clean up found messes

**PLATINUM MEDAL:**
Prevent messes

The beauty of The SINK Project is that we ask each and every individual to sign a certificate that makes a commitment to think about The SINKS all around them every day.

SOMETIMES IT'S

the simplest
encounters

THAT CAN MAKE THE MOST

significant changes

IN YOUR LIFE.

Imagine a company where every employee takes the initiative to act on the needs all around them.

It is very likely that you would see dramatic improvements in productivity, teamwork, and morale.

AND WE
OWE IT ALL

# TO ONE STRANGER

EARLIER
WE
ASKED,

"What would the world look like if we all left things better than we found them?"

THERE IS ONLY ONE WAY TO FIND OUT...

GO
FIND
YOUR
SINK!

83

The largest final step owes its existence to the smallest first step.

— WALTER NUSBAUM

# MY SINK COMMITMENT

I, _____ , commit every day
to leaving people, places, and things better
than I found them!

Signature _____

Date _____

The SINK is not just a philosophy but a service and excellence program. Companies like the Ritz-Carlton are famous for applying principles of excellence within their business. The Ritz has a mantra that says,

> "We are Ladies and Gentlemen serving Ladies and Gentlemen."

## WHAT'S YOURS?

Do you deploy The SINK model within your organization? How about within your life?

This book has the biggest impact when it is read by everyone in your organization.

Bulk pricing is available.

Invest in your team today. Buy a case for your friends, employees and colleagues.

If you'd like to apply The SINK Method to your business teams, training processes, leadership program or to have us speak at your conference, message us today.

www.TheNusbaumGroup.com

www.DarenMartin.com

# A MESSAGE FROM WALTER AND DAREN

You're going to put down this book; however, the next time you go to a bathroom in the airport (or your place of work, your home, or anywhere really) remember these important words – "Leave it better than you found it."

Every time we do something as simple as wiping down a sink, we find others mimicking our behavior. Service starts with you. Be an Impracteur

Are you really authentically making the world around you a better place? Impact Trips to other countries or low-income areas are awesome and produce some great photo opportunities. But what about right where you live?

The law of reciprocity states that when you do something nice for someone else, they will have a deep-rooted urge to do something nice in return.

Just one spark can set the world on fire, so let's get after it and set the world ablaze one small sink at a time!

## WALTER NUSBAUM
Author, Speaker, and Transformation Expert

Walter Nusbaum has spoken to and worked closely with thousands of leaders from all over the world. His core message is that effective transformations require the right actions at the right time. This is where extraordinary success is found. Find him at TheNusbaumGroup.com.

## DAREN MARTIN, PHD,
The Culture Architect, Speaker, Advisor

Daren ran his own company for 20 years. For the last 10 years he has provided transformational consulting for companies ranging in size from small to Fortune 100. He is an in demand keynote speaker who fully engages crowds with action inducing content. Check out his podcast The Daren Martin Show as well as his other books, *A Company of Owners*, *Whiteboard*, and *Beached Whale*. Connect with him at DarenMartin.com.